CONTENTS

WORLD & WHITMAN

Copyright © MCMLXXIX by Metro-Goldwyn-Mayer Inc.
All rights reserved throughout the world.
Published in Great Britain by World Distributors (Manchester) Limited,
A Pentos Company, P.O. Box 111, 12 Lever Street, Manchester M60 1TS,
by arrangement with Western Publishing Company, Inc.,
Racine, Wisconsin, USA.
Printed in Great Britain by Morrison & Gibb Ltd., Edinburgh.
SBN 7235 6553 8

TOM and JERRY

in **DANCING MICE**

5

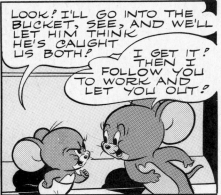

13

SIT DOWN AND TRY TO PULL YOURSELF TOGETHER!

A ROCKIN' CHAIR *IS* SORTA SOOTHIN'!

JERRY, I'LL BET YOU'RE THINKING THE SAME THING AS I AM!

RIGHT!

NOW, DON'T YOU FELLAS DO ANYTHING TO MAKE ME JUMP!

THOMPSON, YOU HAVE OUR SOLEMN PROMISE!

AACH!

CRACK
CRACK

YOU JUST PROMISED...

WELL, YOU DIDN'T *JUMP*, DID YOU?

WE MADE SURE YOU WERE *GLUED* TO YOUR CHAIR!

HOW DO I GET LOOSE?

OH, YOU'LL THINK OF *SOME* WAY!

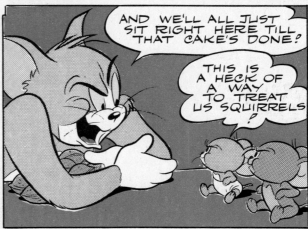

24

Ground Control to BIRDMICE

25

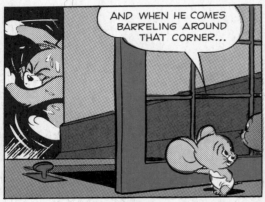

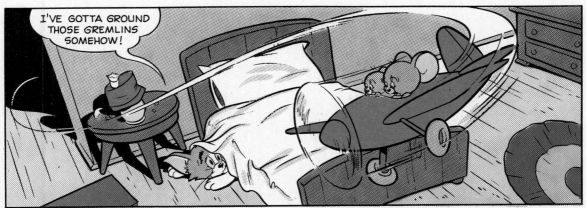

DEEP FREEZER

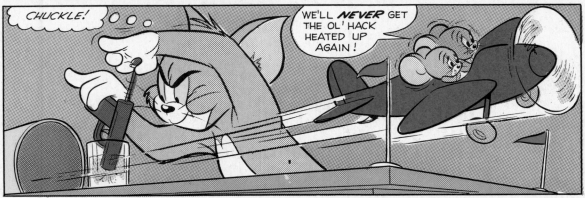

32

33

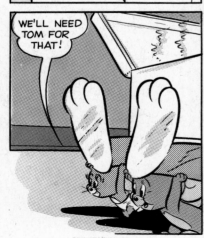

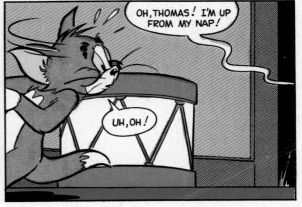

A BIG BAKE·UP

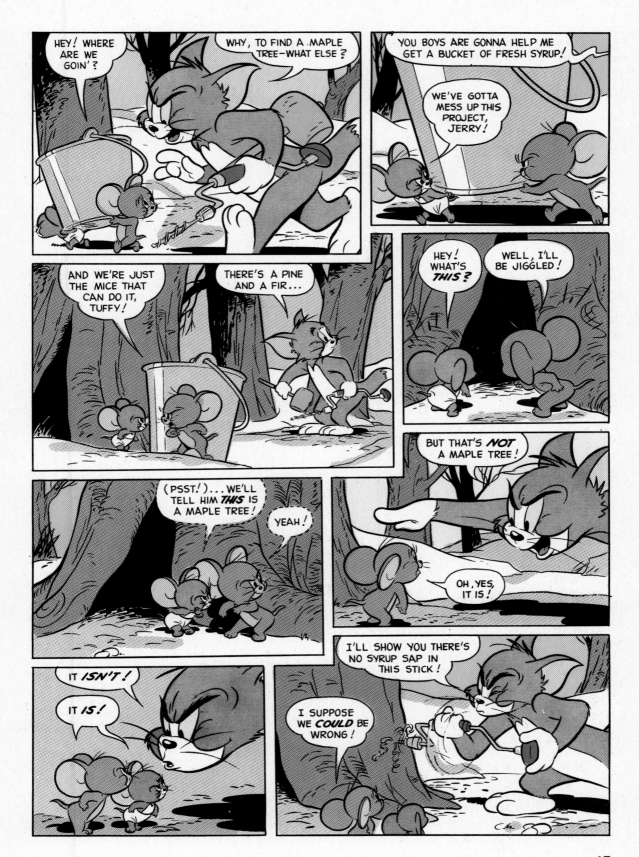

47

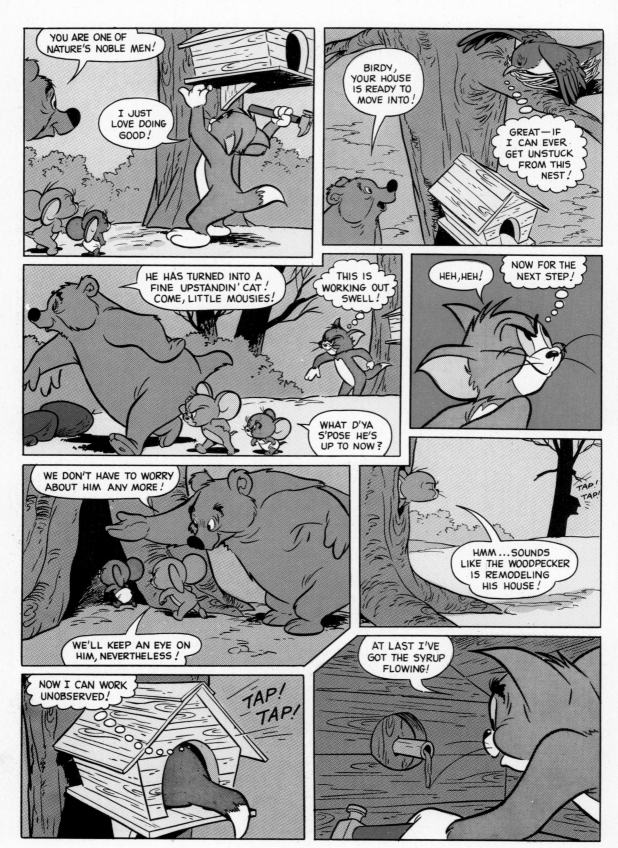

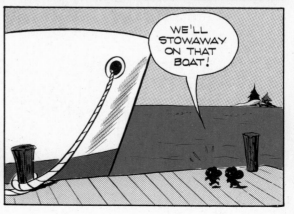